6.13

EQUATORIAL CLIMATES

Keith Lye

RSVP

RAINTREE STECK-VAUGHN
P U B L I S H E R S
The Steck-Vaughn Company

Austin, Texas

Published by Raintree Steck-Vaughn Publishers, an imprint of Steck-Vaughn Company

Library of Congress Cataloging-in-Publication Data
Lye, Keith.
Equatorial climates / Keith Lye.
    p.   cm.—(Climates)
    Includes bibliographical references and index.
    Summary: Describes the weather, plant and animal life, and how people live in the rain forest, monsoon, and savanna regions of the tropics.
    ISBN 0-8172-4826-9
    1. Tropics—Climate—Juvenile literature.
    2. Climatic changes—Tropics—Juvenile literature.
    3. Rain forests—Juvenile literature.
    4. Monsoons—Juvenile literature.
    [1. Tropics—Climates. 2. Climatic changes—Tropics. 3. Climatology. 4. Rain forests.]
    I. Title. II. Series: Lye, Keith. World's climate.
    QC993.5.L94 1997
    551.6913—dc20   96-32758

Printed in Italy. Bound in the United States.
1 2 3 4 5 6 7 8 9 0 0 01 00 99 98 97

Cover picture: Top of the Mahakan River deep in the rain forest of Borneo (Robert Harding)

Picture acknowledgments
Carole Kane: p 17; Edward Parker Photography: pp 12, 13, 26, 37; Frank Lane Picture Agency: pp 9, 10, 14, 15, 18, 33, 35, 36, 39, 41, 43; Keith Lye: pp 16, 27; Lisa Ransom: pp 4, 21; Robert Harding: front cover, pp 1, 7, 13, 14, 17, 19, 21, 23, 27, 28, 31, 32, 34, 36, 39, 40; Tony Stone: p 19; Trip: pp 7, 29, 33, 42; Wayland: pp 28, 29.

Contents

Around the Equator

CLIMATIC REGIONS

Climate is the usual, or average, weather of a place. It determines what kinds of plants and animals are found in an area, and it influences how people live.

The world has four main climates. They are cold climates, equatorial (hot and wet) climates, dry climates, and temperate climates. Temperate climates are not extremely hot, cold, or dry.

Cold climates occur around the North and South Poles. Here, the sun is low in the sky, and its slanted rays are spread over a large area of land. The hottest regions are the tropics, which lie north and south of the equator (the imaginary line that runs around the earth, half-way between the two poles). The tropics form a broad region between the Tropic of Cancer (which is an imaginary line about $23^1/_2$ degrees north of the equator)

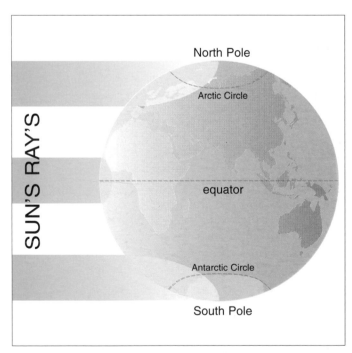

Above *The effect of the sun's rays at the equator and, farther away, at the Poles*

Left *Wet but warm weather conditions at the equator*

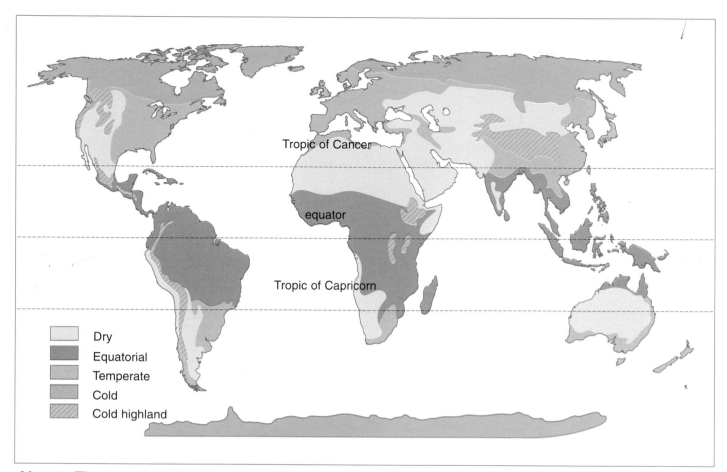

Above *The world's main climate regions*

Dry
Equatorial
Temperate
Cold
Cold highland

and the Tropic of Capricorn (about 23$\frac{1}{2}$ degrees south of the equator).

In the tropics, temperatures are high near sea level. At noon the sun's rays shine almost straight down on the earth's surface. These direct rays produce much more heat than the slanted rays near the poles. The only cool areas in the tropics are highlands. Average temperatures fall by about 1 °F (0.6 °C) for every 300 feet (100m) above sea level.

This book describes places in the tropics with a hot and wet equatorial climate. In some areas, rain occurs throughout the year, and dense rain forests cover the land. Other places have heavy rains, but some months are dry. These are the monsoon regions. A third kind of equatorial climate has a wet season, then a long dry season. The total rainfall is less than in monsoon areas, and the land is covered by savanna—tropical grassland with scattered trees. Hot and wet equatorial climates affect about 20 percent of the world's land area.

RAINFALL RECORDS

People in equatorial regions often get up at dawn to enjoy the cool temperatures. As the sun rises in the sky, the land and air heat up rapidly, and by midday it is extremely hot. Moisture from the land and sea and from lakes and rivers evaporates: it changes from a liquid into an invisible gas called water vapor.

The hot air rises upward in strong currents, carrying water vapor with it. As the air rises, it cools. Cold air cannot hold as much water vapor as warm air, so the vapor condenses (turns back into a liquid or solid), forming tiny droplets of water or crystals of ice.

These are so tiny that they do not fall to the ground but instead form clouds. By mid-afternoon, some clouds are huge and anvil-shaped at the top. These are thunder-clouds, and by late afternoon lightning followed by loud crashes of thunder occurs. The tiny water droplets merge into raindrops, while the ice often forms hailstones. Rainfall formed this way is called convectional rain, and as much as 24 inches (600 mm) can fall in a day.

Another kind of rainfall is orographic rain. This occurs when wind blows up over mountains and the air cools, forming clouds. This is why mountain peaks are often

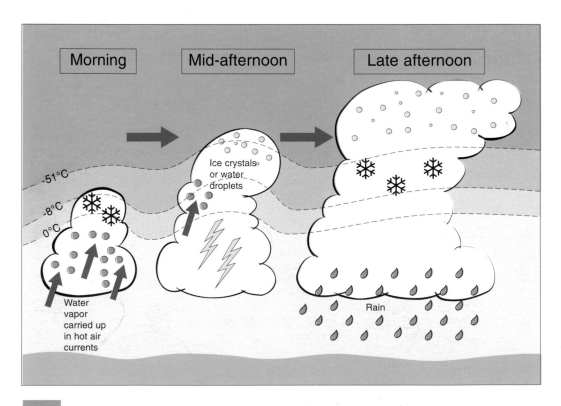

Morning Mid-afternoon Late afternoon

-51°C

-8°C

0°C

Ice crystals or water droplets

Water vapor carried up in hot air currents

Rain

Left How an equatorial thunderstorm develops. In the late morning water vapor rises into the air, and by mid-afternoon it has cooled and formed into clouds that drop heavy rain by late afternoon.

hidden by clouds. Mount Waialeale, the highest peak on the island of Kauai in Hawaii, has orographic rain on a record number of 350 days every year.

The record rainfall for one year is 1,058 inches (26,461 mm) and is held by the village of Cherrapunji in northeastern India. This record was achieved between August 1, 1860 and July 31, 1861. Cherrapunji also holds the record rainfall for one month—372 inches (9,300 mm) in July 1861. Cherrapunji has a seasonal monsoon climate. Most of the rain occurs between the months of May and September.

Above Mount Waialeale, in the Hanarei Valley on Kauai, Hawaii, often has its peaks hidden in clouds.

Right In the middle of each year, these slopes in Darjeeling, India, will get heavy monsoon rains.

HURRICANES

Thunderstorms are common in equatorial regions. But other highly destructive storms hit some coastal regions and islands in the tropics. In North America these storms are called hurricanes. In other parts of the world, people use other names. They are called tropical cyclones in the Indian Ocean, typhoons in the western Pacific Ocean, and willy-willies in northern Australia.

Hurricanes form over the oceans north and south of the equator.

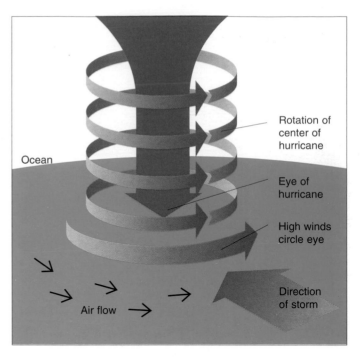

Ocean

Rotation of center of hurricane

Eye of hurricane

High winds circle eye

Direction of storm

Air flow

Above *Cross-section of a hurricane*
Below *Hurricane zones of the world*

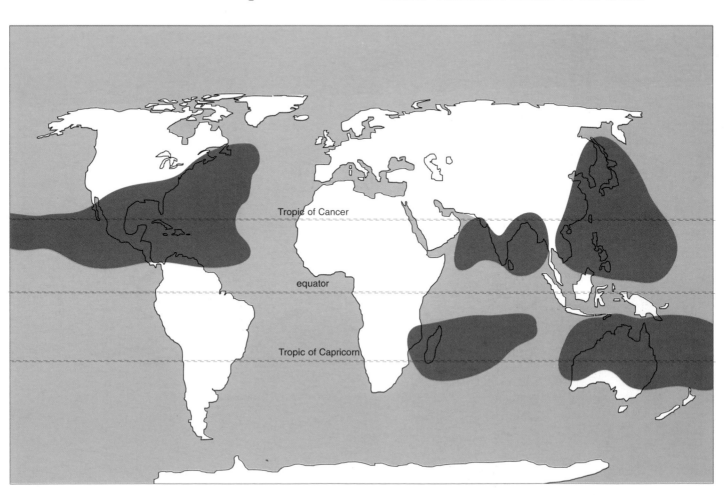

Tropic of Cancer

equator

Tropic of Capricorn

Above *Devastation caused in 1974 when Darwin, Australia, was hit by a hurricane*

From space they look like huge circular spirals of cloud and measure from 120 to 300 miles (200 to 500 km) across. The clouds rotate around a central eye, which is a calm area where air is sinking. But around the eye, hot air containing huge amounts of water vapor rises swiftly upward in strong currents, causing replacement air to be drawn across the oceans toward the center of the storm. This creates strong winds, which may reach speeds of 185 miles per hour (300 km/h).

Hurricanes move from the oceans toward the land. Weather forecasters follow their paths from photographs taken by space satellites. They give warnings to people who live on coasts in the paths of the hurricanes, but no one can prevent the tremendous damage they cause. The Australian city of Darwin was devastated by a willy-willy on Christmas Day, 1974. A tropical cyclone caused floods in Bangladesh in November 1974. About a million people died, many of whom were drowned. Others died later from famine and disease. In 1992, a hurricane hit the southeastern United States causing damage estimated at $22 billion.

Scientists do not know exactly how hurricanes are formed, but it is clear that their energy depends on the huge amounts of water vapor they get from the oceans. When they pass over land, they lose this supply of moisture and soon die out.

Equatorial Rain Forests

HOT AND WET

Large areas of low-lying land north and south of the equator have a hot and wet climate. Temperatures are high in every month, averaging 80 °F (27 °C) or more. There is no winter season. The difference between average temperatures in the warmest and coolest months is often no more than 2–3 °F (1–2 °C). This is far less than the difference between temperatures during the day and at night, which may change by 20 °F (10 °C) or more. As a result, people who live near the equator often say that their winter comes once a day—at night.

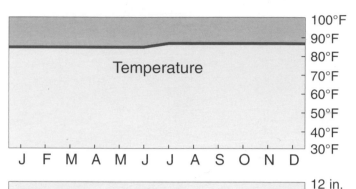

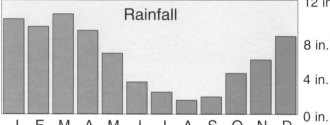

Temperature and rainfall graphs for Manaus, Brazil—a low-lying land south of the equator

Low-lying equatorial regions are also rainy. They seldom have less than 32 inches (800 mm) of rain

Rainstorm in the Amazon basin, South America. The Amazon River basin has an extreme equatorial climate.

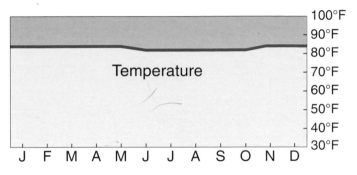

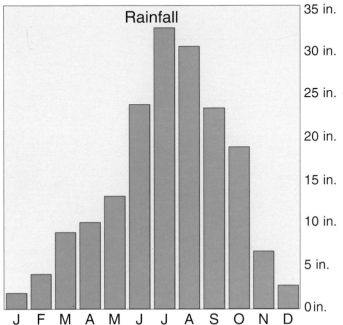

Temperature and rainfall graphs for Douala, Cameroon, West Africa—a hot, wet climate

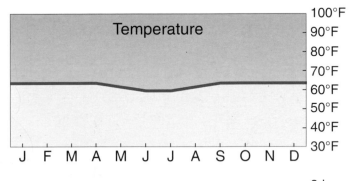

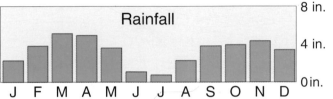

Temperature and rainfall graphs for Kabale, Uganda—away from the extreme equatorial climate of the Zaire basin

every year, while the average yearly rainfall over large areas often exceeds 80 inches (2,000 mm). There is no dry season—some rain falls in every month of the year. Much of the rain comes from thunderstorms, but highlands near the coast also get orographic rain as moist winds from the sea sweep inland.

The two main areas with a hot and wet climate are the Amazon River basin in South America and the Zaire River basin in central Africa. Of these two large regions, the Amazon basin has the most extreme equatorial climate because it is lower and wetter than the Zaire basin. Smaller areas with this kind of climate also occur in Central America, some Caribbean islands, parts of West Africa, eastern Madagascar, and Indonesia.

The hot and wet equatorial climate is generally confined to low-lying areas and is often called the rain forest climate because of the huge forests that grow there. Above 3,000 feet (1,000 m), the average temperatures are lower, and cooler highland climates occur.

People living in equatorial lowlands often travel to the highlands to seek relief from the lowland weather conditions, which are always uncomfortably hot and humid.

RAIN FOREST PLANTS

Rain forests are usually rather dark places because very little sunlight reaches the wet and muddy floor. The only places where tangles of undergrowth grow on the ground are in forest clearings or along river banks. The roof of the forest, which consists of the crowns of the trees, is known as the canopy. It is here that the richest growth of plants occurs.

Most trees in rain forests are evergreens and grow from 15 to 65 feet (5 to 20 m) high. The tallest of the trees, with an average height of 130 feet (40 m), can reach 325 feet (100 m).

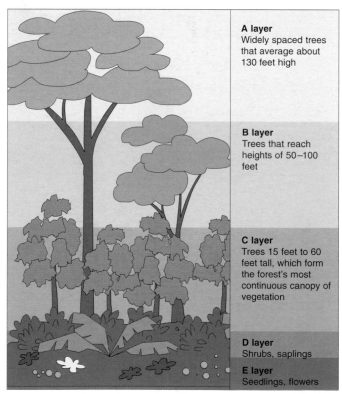

A layer
Widely spaced trees that average about 130 feet high

B layer
Trees that reach heights of 50–100 feet

C layer
Trees 15 feet to 60 feet tall, which form the forest's most continuous canopy of vegetation

D layer
Shrubs, saplings

E layer
Seedlings, flowers

Rain Forest Layers

Because of the unchanging hot and wet climate, the rain forests are rich in plant species. An area as small as two or three acres often contains as many as 150 species of trees. In a similar area of temperate forest in Europe or the United States, there are only about 10 species. Most rain forest trees have slender, straight trunks, and the branches grow near the tops of the trunks.

Plant parasites, called epiphytes, are common in rain forests. These plants, which include ferns, orchids, mosses, and lichens, live on other plants. Flowering plants called

Above *The Amazon rain forest from the air*

Right *Inside the rain forest*

bromeliads grow on other plants, taking their moisture and food directly from the air or from decaying plants nearby. The rosettes of their leaves trap raindrops, storing water high above the ground. Small animals, such as frogs and spiders, often live in these tiny pools. Some epiphytes send roots down to the forest floor and become self-supporting.

Others, called stranglers, kill the trees that once supported them.

Another group of plants are climbers, or lianas. These woody plants are rooted in the forest floor, but they climb toward the upper layers of the forest using the trees for support. Many epiphytes and climbers compete for space with the branches and leaves of the canopy.

RAIN FOREST ANIMALS

Rain forests cover only about 6 percent of the world's land surface but, because of the hot, wet climate, they contain more than half of the world's plant and animal species. Scientists have estimated that, on average, an area of 40,000 square miles (100,000 km^2) contains up to 750 tree species and 1,500 species of flowering plants.

The same area is home to about 400 species of birds, 100 species of reptiles, and 60 species of amphibians. There are great numbers of insects, including beautiful butterflies, beetles, ants, and termites. Insects are important because they help to clear the forest of dead plant matter. Some ants cut up leaves and use the material to make food for their larvae. Termites live in dead wood and help it to decompose.

Compared with the savanna regions bordering the rain forests, the number of mammal species is relatively low. Most of them, including monkeys and flying squirrels, can move easily and quickly through the forest canopy, which is rich in plant foods. Many of these animals never come down to the ground. One strange animal in the rain forests of South

Above *Leafcutter ants in Guyana clear the forest of dead plant matter.*

Left *The mitered leaf monkey lives high in the rain forest canopy.*

Right *An ocelot from South America*

America is the sloth. This animal spends most of its life hanging upside down from branches.

Some heavy primates, such as chimpanzees and gorillas, live mostly on the forest floor. Other forest floor animals include deer, antelope, anteaters, and wild pigs. They feed on roots, seeds, leaves, and fruits that fall from the trees. One rare animal found on the forest floor in central Africa is the okapi, a relative of the giraffe. Animals that hunt include several large cats, such as leopards in Africa and jaguars and ocelots in South America. Large snakes and birds of prey also feed on smaller animals.

AMAZONIAN FOREST DWELLERS

The Amazon River basin contains the world's largest rain forest. This region is the home of Amerindian peoples, whose ancestors arrived from North America around 15,000 years ago.

Before the arrival of European explorers nearly 500 years ago, the Amerindian people lived in total harmony with their surroundings. When they wanted to set up a village, they cleared a patch of land where they built houses and farmed the land. Some villages consisted of a cluster of houses, one for each family, while others contained just one large house, called a maloca, which held up to 150 people.

Around their homes, the people grew crops, including their main food, cassava, from which tapioca is made. But soil exposed to the weather soon becomes infertile because the heavy rain washes out the chemicals that plants need to grow. When the land became infertile, the people cleared a new plot. The forest soon grew back over the abandoned land.

The Amerindians had a deep knowledge of the rain forest. From it they obtained many foods and also plants they used as medicines.

Left Amazonian Indians with blowpipes outside a maloca

Top right A young hunter in Brazil with a bow and arrow

Bottom right A canoe made from a hollowed out tree trunk

16

More than 100 plants were used to make poisons. Hunters and fishermen used the poisons on the tips of their spears and darts.

Contact with Europeans proved a disaster for the Amerindians and has led to the extinction of about 90 groups. Many of them were badly treated and some were forced into slavery. The people also lacked resistance to common European diseases and this led to many deaths. In the last 100 years, outsiders have begun to exploit the forest, cutting down large areas to make way for cattle ranches, mines, and reservoirs.

AFRICAN AND ASIAN FOREST DWELLERS

Central Africa contains the world's second largest rain forest. Among its oldest inhabitants are pygmies who live in small bands, hunting animals and gathering food from wild plants. The pygmies once occupied a much larger area, but other Africans have moved into the forest, cutting down trees, building villages, and setting up farms.

Some pygmies have given up their hunting and gathering way of life and work as laborers in the villages, but others still depend entirely on the forest. They call the forest their "mother and father" and perform ceremonies to ensure that they have friendly relations with the natural world.

One group of pygmies, called the Mbuti, lives in the Ituri forest in northeastern Zaire. They trade forest products with the village people, exchanging such things as wild honey, meat, and mushrooms for metal tools and cast-off clothes. In this way, they are able to live in their forest, which supplies all their other needs. The Mbuti build shelters from branches thatched with large leaves to keep out the rain. They make cloth from tree

Left Mbuti pygmies in a central African forest making arrows and poison

Top right Forest people in New Guinea

Bottom right Oxen being used to move logs in Burma, Southeast Asia

bark, which they smoke over a fire and then hammer out to shape it.

Other forest peoples live in Southeast Asia and on some Pacific islands. They include negritos, who resemble pygmies. Many negritos have abandoned the hunting and gathering way of life, but some remote groups still continue this ancient lifestyle. Like the pygmies, their beliefs are closely linked to nature. Some of them worship nature gods, such as the powerful thunder-god.

Some forest people on the island of New Guinea farm plots of land until the soil is exhausted, much like the Amerindians in South America. But some of the Punan people of Borneo are constantly moving and wander through the rain forests. They hunt using blowpipes tipped with poison and also train dogs to help them.

Monsoon Climates

CHANGING SEASONS

Unlike equatorial climates that are hot and wet throughout the year, monsoon climates are marked by two main seasons. For about half of the year, winds blow from the oceans onto the land. These moist winds bring rain, especially in places where the winds are forced to rise over mountain ranges. For the other six months, winds blow from the land toward the sea. This is the dry (or drier) season.

Monsoon climates are a halfway stage between hot and wet equatorial climates and savanna climates. The total amount of rainfall that falls during the rainy season in monsoon regions is often greater than the total yearly rainfall in the hot and wet equatorial regions. But the dry season is not as long or as severe as in savanna climates. The soil, just below the surface, remains moist during the whole of the dry season. As a result, forests can grow in monsoon regions. This makes them different from the tropical grasslands with scattered trees, which are typical of savanna climates.

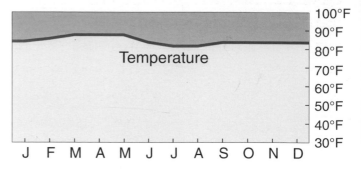

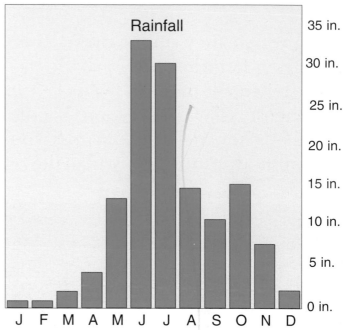

Temperature and rainfall graphs for Cochin, India. This monsoon climate is halfway between an equatorial and a savanna climate.

The word monsoon comes from the Arabic "mausim" which means "season." Arab sailors used this word for the winds in the Arabian Sea. For about six months every year, these winds blow from the southwest. For the other six months they blow from the northeast.

20

Today, we use the term "monsoon climate" for any area where winds completely change direction from season to season. Monsoons occur mainly in the tropics, notably in parts of Central and South America, parts of Africa, Southeast Asia, and northern Australia. Monsoon winds even occur in some temperate regions, including northeastern Asia. But the best known of all monsoons occur in the Indian subcontinent. This region includes Pakistan, India, Bangladesh, Nepal, Bhutan, and Sri Lanka. Here, life is determined by the seasons.

Right *A baking hot scene in northern India (March–May) before the monsoon*

Below *Storm clouds advancing during the Indian monsoon*

THE INDIAN MONSOON

In the winter, the highlands north of India are cold and the air is chilled. Cold air is dense (heavy) and sinks down to the earth's surface. This sinking air creates a huge region of high air pressure. At the same time, the opposite is happening south of India, around the equator. Here the air is warmed and expands. As a result it becomes lighter and rises, creating a zone of low air pressure called the doldrums.

Air moves from the high pressure area in the north toward the low air pressure zone in the south. Because the earth is spinning, the air does not flow directly north to south. Instead it is deflected, moving generally from the northeast toward the southwest. These currents of air are called the northeast trade winds.

Northern India is dry and relatively cool from late December until early March. The land then heats up rapidly, creating a region of low air pressure over the land, which starts to draw in air from the sea. From June on, the wind direction is turned around. Air from trade winds that blow toward the equator in the southern hemisphere is drawn northward by low pressure over Northern India. These winds veer to become southwest winds in the Arabian Sea and southeast winds in the Bay of Bengal.

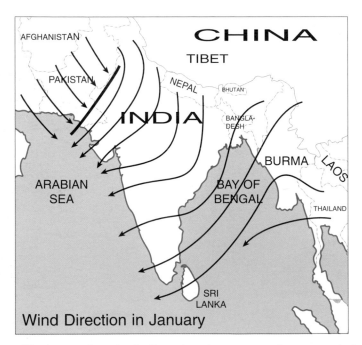

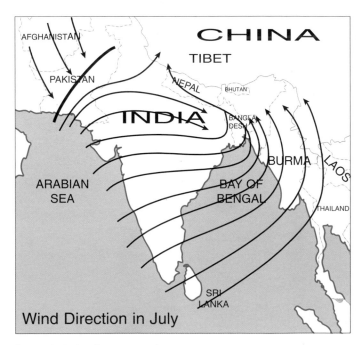

Changes in wind direction between January (winter) and July (summer)

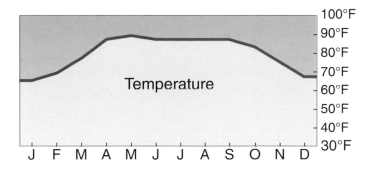

Temperature

100°F
90°F
80°F
70°F
60°F
50°F
40°F
30°F

J F M A M J J A S O N D

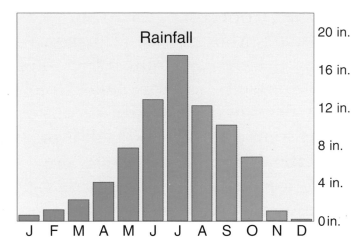

Rainfall

20 in.

16 in.

12 in.

8 in.

4 in.

0 in.

J F M A M J J A S O N D

These monsoon winds, which are sucked into the low air-pressure region over the Indian sub-continent, have picked up huge amounts of water vapor during their passage over the warm oceans. As the winds reach land, the water vapor is converted into clouds and rainstorms. The rainfall is heavy along India's west coast, but the wettest places are in northeastern India. Here, the village of Mawsynram, in the state of Meghalaya, holds the record for being the wettest place in the world. It has an average yearly rainfall of 475 inches (11,873 mm).

Above *Temperature and rainfall graphs for Dhaka, Bangladesh, show the effect the monsoon winds have as they reach northeastern India in July.*

Left *Wind directions in January and July*

Right *Heavy rain from the monsoon in Dhaka during July*

THE AUSTRALIAN MONSOON

Northern Australia lies in the tropics and has a monsoon climate. There are two main seasons—the warm, dry winters last from May to October and the hot, wet summer months run from November to April.

In the winter, southeast trade winds blow from the interior, across northern Australia toward the seas in the north. These dry winds are drawn northward toward the doldrums, the low air-pressure zone located around the equator to the north.

In the summer, the interior of Australia is intensely heated. The northeast trade winds, which blow toward the equator in the northern hemisphere, are drawn southward and veer to become northwest winds. These winds, which have picked up huge amounts of moisture from the sea, blow on-shore bringing heavy rain to coastal towns such as Darwin, which is in what the Australians call the "Top End" of the Northern Territory. The northern coasts also lie in the paths of willy-willies (hurricanes)

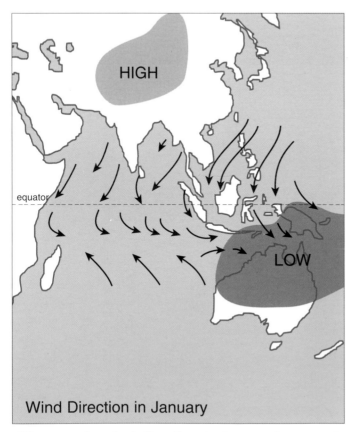

Wind Direction in January

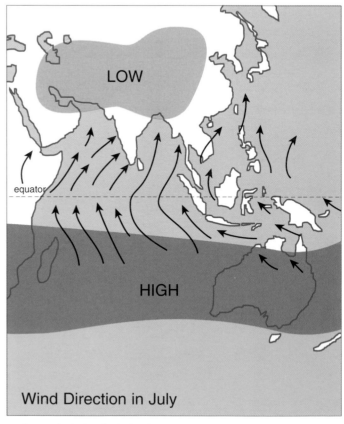

Wind Direction in July

Changes in wind direction between January (summer) and July (winter)

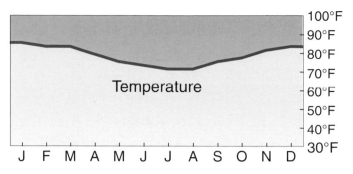

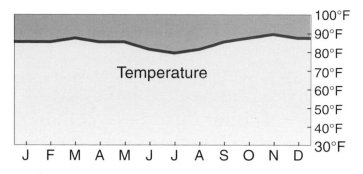

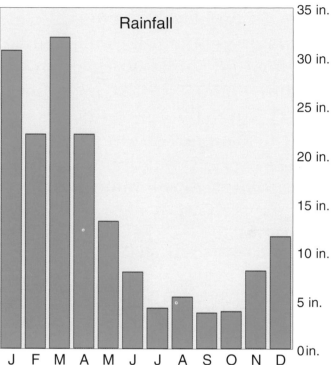

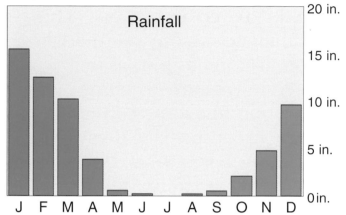

Temperature and rainfall graphs for Darwin. The northwest winds bring heavy rain during the summer.

that form over the seas north of Australia. Inland the rainfall gradually diminishes. As a result, the monsoon forests in the coastal regions of northern Australia merge southward into grassy woodlands and, eventually, deserts.

The northeast coast of Queensland, especially the area around Cairns, is even wetter than the north coasts. It has rain in every month of the year, although the wettest months are in summer (January, February, and March). Much of the rain on the northeastern coast comes from the moist southeast trade winds that

Cairns, on Australia's east coast, has rain every month of the year.

blow onshore. Other rains come from willy-willies, which often bring destructive gale-force winds. Tropical forests grow along the Queensland coast, but the rainfall diminishes inland and the tropical forests merge into wooded savanna. The Great Dividing Range, which separates the coastal plains from the interior, acts as a barrier against the moist onshore winds.

PLANTS AND ANIMALS

In appearance, tropical monsoon forests are much like the rain forests. They have a canopy formed by the branches and leaves at the tops of trees about 100 feet (30 m) above ground level. There is also an understory, containing such plants as palms and bamboo, which grow in dense clumps. Herbs, including grasses, cover the forest floor.

Because monsoon forests have a dry season every year, they have fewer trees than the rain forests.

They also contain fewer parasitic epiphytes and tangled climbing plants. Another difference is that the trees are not all evergreens. Several trees, such as the valuable sal and teak, are deciduous. They shed their leaves during the dry season, not in autumn as in temperate regions.

Monsoon forests are often damaged by fire, especially during the dry season. Forest fires, together with logging, have modified much

Monsoon rain forest near Cairns, Australia

Elephants in an elephant orphanage in southern Sri Lanka

A Bengal tiger in India having a drink of water

of the monsoon forest where trees and plants are renewed more often than in the rain forests. They are also generally more open to sunlight.

The animals of the monsoon forests are of the same types as in the hot and wet rain forests. Most species, including monkeys and other primates, are adapted to live in the trees. The most famous predator in the monsoon forests of the Indian subcontinent is the Bengal tiger, although hunters have killed so many of them that they are close to extinction. Another animal now rare in the wild is the Indian elephant. The majority are tame, and they are used by loggers as beasts of burden, hauling tree trunks from the forests.

PEOPLE IN MONSOON AREAS

Farming is the chief activity in southern Asia, and rice is the main crop. One kind of rice, called wet paddy, grows best on swampy plains in water up to 6 inches (15 cm) deep. Wet tropical climates, with high temperatures and a yearly rainfall of more than 45 inches (1,200 mm), are ideal for wet paddy.

In monsoon areas, farmers prepare their land during the dry season, building ridges around the fields. These ridges hold in the water when the field is flooded. The farmers also repair the irrigation channels around the fields. These channels are used to drain off excess water. Meanwhile,

Above *Villagers planting and tending rice in Indonesia*

Left *An Indian city in rainy weather*

Top right *A rice farmer from Jakarta in Indonesia*

Right *An Aboriginal hunter from Melville Island, Australia*

young rice seedlings are grown in nurseries.

When the monsoon rains arrive, the fields are flooded and everyone works hard to transplant the seedlings in the wet ground. This work is usually done by hand. The plants then grow for 4 to 5 months. The fields are drained before the harvest, which takes place after the end of the rainy season.

Some of the world's most densely populated regions, including the plains of Bangladesh, lie in the monsoon regions of southern Asia. The people depend so much on the climate that, if the monsoon winds fail to bring enough rain, the crops will fail. If the rains are unusually heavy, then floods occur. In both of these cases, the crops are lost and the people are faced with starvation.

Another group of people who live in a monsoon region are the Aboriginal people of northern Australia. These people, who are descended from the first human inhabitants of Australia, live by hunting animals, such as kangaroos, and collecting plant foods. Several areas in Arnhem Land in Northern Territory are now protected reserves. In these areas the Aboriginal people carry on their traditional way of life.

Savanna Climates

WET AND DRY

The third type of equatorial climate is the savanna climate. This climate is known for its distinct wet and dry seasons. It is warm or hot throughout the year, and average temperatures are similar to those in other equatorial climates. But the yearly temperature range (the difference between average temperatures in the warmest and coolest month) is usually greater. As a result, people in savanna regions sometimes say that they have three, rather than two, seasons. These are a cooler dry season, a hotter dry season before the start of the rains, and a hot wet season, marked by violent thunderstorms and strong winds.

The total rainfall in savanna regions is usually much less than in the other rainy equatorial regions. The typical average annual rainfall is between 32 and 60 inches (800 and 1,500 mm), but the rainfall is much less reliable and seasonal

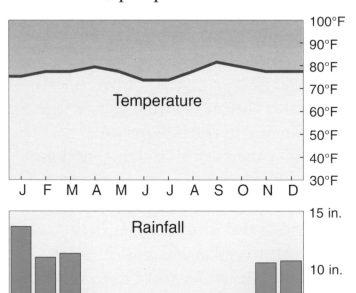

The rainfall graph for Goiás, Brazil, shows the dry season from May to August.

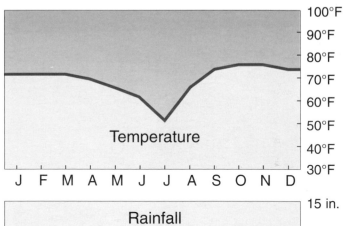

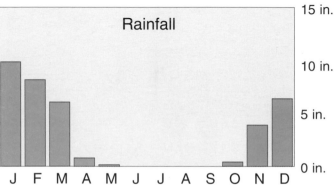

Temperature and rainfall graphs for Lusaka, Zambia, show the seasonal temperature.

African savanna in Kenya. The clouds are hovering over the high ground.

differences are much more marked. For example, in Lusaka, capital of Zambia, the average annual rainfall is 33 inches (836 mm). Only about 1 inch (31 mm) comes in the winter months, between May and October. The remaining 32 inches (805 mm) fall in the summer months, between October and March. The wettest month is January.

In Africa, the savanna regions lie between the equatorial rain forests and the dry and desert regions to the north and south. There is no clear boundary between the regions.

Around the equatorial rain forests, the trees gradually thin out before merging into the true savanna, which consists of tropical grassland with scattered trees. But forests still persist in wet areas, such as river valleys. While the subsoil in monsoon regions remains moist during the dry season, enabling trees to grow, the soil in savanna regions dries out. The soil cracks and winds blow dust into the air. Smoke from grass fires also often fills the air, and rivers are reduced to little more than a trickle of water.

PLANT LIFE

The main plants in savanna regions are coarse grasses, small trees, and shrubs. Some open grasslands in tropical Africa are dotted with larger trees, such as flat-topped acacias and swollen-trunked baobabs. They resemble parklands, but they are rarely as green as parks in temperate lands. The grasses often grow in clumps, with bare soil between the patches of grass. In the dry season, the landscape is parched and brown.

The area covered by trees and shrubs depends mainly on the length of the wet season. Moist tree savanna, which often resembles woodland, grows in regions with a wet season lasting seven to nine months or more. In wet areas, elephant grasses grow to heights of 16 feet (5 m) and trees are numerous. Places with a shorter wet season have a dry tree savanna, with fewer trees and shorter grasses, up to 30 inches (80 cm) in height. When the wet season is even shorter —between three and four months long—thorn savanna (grassland with thorny bushes) is common.

In all savanna regions, plants must be adapted to survive the dry season. Generally, trees are small and deciduous, shedding their

A baobab tree, which stores water to keep alive during the dry season

Right *Flat-topped acacia trees in the savanna in Serengeti National Park, Tanzania*

Left *This savanna landscape is in Tanzania, Africa.*

leaves during the dry season. They have deep roots to tap moisture well below the surface. The leaves of grasses also die off at the start of the dry season, but the sheaths from the dead leaves protect the tissue that produces the new shoots, which spring to life as soon as the rains start.

The largest savanna regions are found in Africa. The savanna in Venezuela, in northern South America, is called the *llanos*, a Spanish word meaning "plains." The savanna in Brazil, south of the Amazon rain forest, is called the *campos*. Savanna regions also occur in India and in the monsoon lands of northern Australia, where eucalyptus trees are common.

ANIMAL LIFE

The African savanna is one of the world's greatest habitats for wild animals. Huge herds roam across the savanna, grazing on the grasses or browsing on the bushes and trees. They include antelope, buffalo, giraffes, and zebras. Elephants and rhinoceroses are also found, though their numbers have been greatly reduced in recent years. Even so, no other region in the world has as many ungulates (hoofed, plant-eating mammals) as the African savanna.

The savanna also has animals that prey on the ungulates. They include cheetahs (the world's fastest animal runners), wild dogs, hyenas, jackals, leopards, and lions. Primates include baboons and monkeys, which live in patches of woodland, while rivers and swamps contain crocodiles and hippopotamuses. The savanna is also rich

Left *A giraffe grazing on the top layer of a tree in Kenya*

Right *Zebras in Zimbabwe*

Far right *Geoldi's Marmoset from South America*

in birds, including bustards, flamingoes, guinea fowl, ostriches (the world's largest living birds), storks, and vultures.

The African savanna once contained far more wild animals, but over-hunting and competition with farmers, who have destroyed large areas of natural habitats, have reduced the populations. Some species are now close to extinction.

The South American *llanos* contains various burrowing animals and a great variety of birds. There are also anteaters, armadillos, burrowing birds, capybaras (the world's largest rodents), jaguars, and tapirs. Most mammals nest in the patches of forest that break up the grasslands and only go to the *llanos* to feed.

Savanna animals in India include the nilgai (a horse-like antelope) and the four-horned antelope. Hares and gerbils are also common, but most predators, including the Indian lion, have been hunted to extinction or forced into remote areas. Familiar animals on the savanna lands of Australia include wallabies and kangaroos, notably the antilopine kangaroo of northern Australia.

PEOPLE OF THE SAVANNA

The world's savanna regions provide large areas for cattle ranching. In Venezuela, the cowboys who work in the *llanos* region are known as *llaneros*. The *llaneros* also farm in areas where there is water available for irrigation of the land.

In Africa, several groups of people are known for raising cattle and other livestock, including goats and sheep. The Fulani in the savanna lands of West Africa are nomadic herders who move from place to place in search of pasture. In East Africa, the Masai herd their animals into an enclosure at night to keep them safe from predators, such as lions. Some Masai families own several hundred animals—the wealth and importance of these people is measured by the number of animals they own. Such large herds overgraze the land, destroying habitats once used by wild animals.

The main restriction on animal raising in Africa is the tsetse fly, which breeds in moist woodland savanna areas. This fly spreads sleeping sickness and a deadly animal disease called nagana. It infests about 3.8 million square miles (10 million km^2) of land north and south of the equator.

Left *The wide expanse of the* llanos *in Venezuela*

Right *A sugarcane plantation in northeast Brazil*

Below *A Masai herdsman in Africa*

Farming is difficult because of the lack of water and the poor soils. Some people who farm move every few years. They clear an area and burn the trees and shrubs. The ash is then used to make the soil fertile. Crops such as cassava, corn, millet, peanuts, and sorghum are grown for a few years. When the soil becomes infertile, the farmers then move to a new plot. This method of farming is being replaced in many areas by more permanent farms using modern methods, such as fertilizers and irrigation. Only a few savanna farms produce crops for sale. Most people are subsistence farmers, producing only enough to meet their families' needs.

The Changing Rain Forest

THE CHANGING FORESTS

Rain forests cover about 6 percent of the world's land areas, but they are disappearing rapidly. Loggers are cutting down trees to sell the lumber, farmers have cleared the trees to create cattle ranches, miners are removing valuable ores, and engineers have flooded large areas to create huge reservoirs to provide new water supplies.

In the mid-1990s, scientists estimated that the tropical forests were being cut back by about 1 percent each year. As a result, more than 20,000 living species are probably becoming extinct every year, many of which have never been studied. Forest clearance creates many other problems. For example, heavy rain washes away the chemicals that make the forest soils fertile. Cleared land soon becomes infertile.

The destruction of tropical forests may also be causing global warming. Global warming is caused by "greenhouse" gases, such as carbon dioxide, in the air. Greenhouse gases act much like the glass in a greenhouse. They let the sun's rays through, but they trap some of the heat that is reflected back into the air from the earth's surface. The higher the volume of greenhouse gases in the atmosphere, the hotter the climate becomes. The burning of the tropical forests is increasing the amount of carbon dioxide that is present in the air. The ongoing destruction of the forests is removing the trees and green plants that take the carbon dioxide from the air.

South and Central America's Threatened Forests

Left Open-cast mining in the Papua New Guinea rain forest

Below Forest destruction has left this hillside bare of trees.

Scientists from all over the world want to halt forest destruction, but most people who live in tropical South America, Africa, and Asia are poor. Many of them favor forest removal, hoping that it will help them to find work and raise the living standards of their families. Another way has to be found to help these people—or forest destruction is bound to continue.

LAND DESTRUCTION

People around the world suffer when natural disasters occur. News bulletins often report on floods in the monsoon regions of Asia or droughts in the savanna regions of Africa.

Floods occur in monsoon regions when heavy rains fill rivers and make them overflow. Human interference with the land can make flooding more damaging and more frequent, as occurs when forests are removed from the slopes of highlands in monsoon regions. Forest soils normally soak up much of the rain, but when the forests are burned or cut down, more water flows across the surfaces of the slopes. This quickly swells the streams that feed the rivers on the plains.

The water flowing over the land picks up bits of soil, making the water muddy. This mud is swept

Soil erosion near Cape Town, South Africa

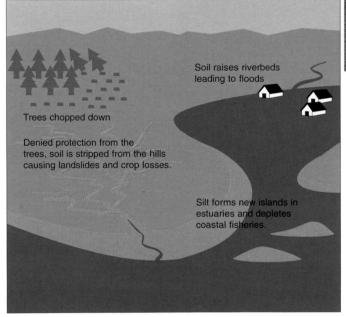

Soil raises riverbeds
leading to floods

Trees chopped down

Denied protection from the
trees, soil is stripped from the hills
causing landslides and crop losses.

Silt forms new islands in
estuaries and depletes
coastal fisheries.

away by the fast-flowing streams
and, on the plains, some of this
mud settles on the riverbeds. This
reduces the depth of the rivers and
increases the danger of flooding.

The rapid removal of soil by
nature, often caused by human
interference, is called soil erosion.
Soil erosion is a serious problem in
tropical regions, including the
savanna. In many parts of the
savanna, people have exposed the
soil by farming, grazing large herds
of animals, and cutting down trees
and bushes to use as firewood.

Exposed soil in savanna regions
is open to the wind during the
long dry season. The wind blows
the soil into the air, causing
choking duststorms. Soil erosion by
the wind becomes worse when long
droughts occur, perhaps lasting
several years and making the soil
extremely dry and powdery. Soil
erosion also occurs when the rains
return. Large raindrops strike the
ground with great force, breaking
up the soil. Running water then
washes away the loose grains. Soil
erosion has turned many once-
fertile areas into barren areas of
bare rock.

CONSERVATION

Learning about climate helps us to understand our world and the plants and animals that live upon it. The study of climate also helps us to realize why disasters occur and how their effects might be reduced. For example, the governments of many countries now realize the danger of global warming. They are working together to control the amount of carbon dioxide getting into the air.

Ordinary people, young and old, have formed groups to learn about how human interference with nature is changing the climate and damaging our planet. Many have campaigned in favor of saving the rain forests and against the destruction of the habitats of wild animals. Scientists explain to the local people how conservation can benefit them. For example, the endangered gorillas in Africa's rain forests are a tourist attraction. By saving the gorillas, the local people can find valuable jobs in the tourist industry.

Conservationists have inspired a world-wide movement to set up national parks, where plants, animals, and beautiful scenery can

be protected so that they can be enjoyed by people for all time. Yellowstone National Park was set up in 1872 in the United States and was the world's first national park.

Since then, national parks have been set up in many other areas, including about 50 African countries. Tropical Africa faces many problems arising from the rapidly increasing population and demands for space for farming, industry, and mining. Yet by 1990, about 4 percent of Africa was protected to some extent. Many of the 600 or so sites are totally protected, while others are partly protected. Partly protected areas can be enjoyed by tourists and some activities, such as logging or mining, are allowed. Conservation policies give us hope that some of Africa's great wildlife habitats may be saved from destruction.

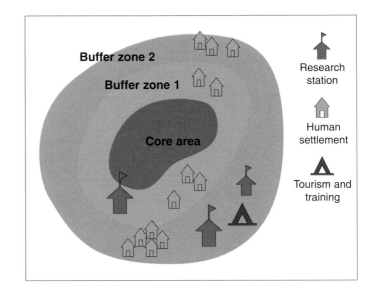

Left *The Masai Mara national park in Kenya*

Top right *An example of the protected areas in a national park and the activities that might be allowed in each*

Right *A visitor with a local guide viewing the rare mountain gorillas*

Glossary

Air pressure Air pressure is produced by the weight of the air above us in the atmosphere. High air pressure occurs when cold, dense air sinks downward. Low air pressure occurs when warm air rises.

Atmosphere The layer of air around the earth.

Carbon dioxide A colorless, odorless gas found in the atmosphere. Green plants need carbon dioxide to live and grow. Animals breathe in oxygen and breathe out carbon dioxide. Carbon dioxide is released when coal, oil, and natural gas are burned.

Celsius The Celsius scale, named after the Swedish scientists Anders Celsius, is used to measure temperature. The freezing point of water is 0 °C. Boiling point is 100 °C.

Conservation Protecting and preserving animals and plants, the soil, old buildings, and so on.

Deciduous trees Trees that lose leaves at some point of the year, such as in autumn or at the start of a dry season, and later grow new leaves.

Drought A long period when the rainfall is well below average.

Equator A line of latitude running around the world exactly halfway between the North and the South poles.

Erosion The wearing away of the land by natural forces. Soil erosion caused by human interference with nature occurs much more quickly than natural erosion.

Evaporation Evaporation occurs when a liquid becomes a vapor or a gas.

Evergreen A shrub or tree that remains in leaf throughout the year.

Fahrenheit Scale used to measure temperature. The freezing point of water is 32 degrees Fahrenheit (32 °F), and the boiling point is 212 degrees Fahrenheit (212 °F).

Fertilizers Manure or chemicals added to the soil to improve crop production.

Habitat The natural home of a plant or animal.

Irrigation The watering of the land by artificial methods, including canals and ditches.

Lightning Huge sparks of electricity in clouds.

Lines of Latitude Lines running around the earth parallel to the equator. Lines of latitude are measured in degrees between the equator (0 °) and the poles (90 ° North and South). Lines of longitude run around the world at right angles to lines of latitude.

Logging The cutting down, trimming, and transportation of trees.

Nomad A person who moves from place to place in search of pasture or food.

Ore A valuable mineral containing metals or other similarly valuable substances.

Predator An animal that preys upon other animals.

Reservoir A place where water is stored. It may be artificial, such as the reservoirs that form behind constructed dams, or it may be a natural phenomenon.

Space satellite An artificial device orbiting the earth or another planet. Weather satellites relay information from space about the weather on the ground.

Species A group of closely related plants or animals. Members of a species can breed together.

Swamp A waterlogged area of ground.

Temperature The measurement of how hot or cold something is.

Thunder The sound made when the air in the path of a stroke of lightning is suddenly expanded by the heat of the lightning.

Water vapor Invisible moisture in the atmosphere.

Weather The day-to-day condition of the atmosphere.

Weather forecaster A person who uses information from weather stations to predict the weather.

Further Information

Books

Jenike, David and Mark Jenike. *A Walk Through the Rain Forest: Life in the Ituri Forest of Zaire.* Cincinnati Zoo Books. New York: Franklin Watts, 1994.

Morrison, Marion. The Amazon Rain Forest and its People. New York: Thomson Learning, 1993.

Miller, Christine G. and Louise A. Berry. *Jungle Rescue: Saving the New World Tropical Rain Forests.* New York: Atheneum Books for Young Readers, 1991.

National Geographic staff. *The Emerald Realm: Earth's Precious Rain Forests.* Washington, DC: National Geographic Society, 1990.

Pope, Joyce. *Plants of the Tropics.* Plant Life Series. New York: Facts on File, 1990.

CD-Rom

Habitats. Steck-Vaughn Interactive, 1996.

Index

Bold numbers indicate illustrations